The Ta...

Heather Hammonds

Contents

Taste Buds

Look at the little bumps on my tongue.
Taste buds are inside the little bumps.

We taste the foods we eat
with our taste buds.

A Taste Test

We did a taste test.

We wanted to find the foods

that we liked best.

Mum helped us.

First we made a taste book.

Sweet Foods

We tasted some cake, fruit and honey.

The cake, fruit and honey tasted sweet.

I liked the cake.

I liked the **icing**

on the cake.

Josh liked the fruit.

Sour Foods

Mum made us
some fish and chips.
Then we put some sour foods
on our fish and chips.

We liked lemon
on our fish and chips.
It made the fish and chips
taste good.

Salty Foods

Next we tasted some crackers, popcorn and pizza.

All the foods had **salt** on them.

I liked the popcorn.

Josh liked the pizza.

	Liked
Sweet foods	Fruit and cake
Sour foods	Lemon on our fish and chips
Salty foods	Pizza and popcorn

We put lots of salt
on the foods.
They did not taste good
at all.

Bitter Foods

Some foods are bitter.

We do not like bitter foods.

Mum said that she can make bitter foods taste good.

Mum put some onion
in a **salad sandwich**.
She said that the onion
tasted good
in the sandwich.

Chocolate Cake

We looked at all the foods
in our taste book.

	Liked
Sweet foods	Fruit and cake
Sour foods	Lemon on our fish and chips
Salty foods	Pizza and popcorn
Bitter foods	Onion in a sandwich (Mum)

Then Mum made us
a chocolate cake.
We liked the taste
of the chocolate cake
best of all!

Glossary

icing

salad sandwich

salt